Yes, Even **You** Can Be A Country Person

*"With Boots, a Hat and This Book-
You Can Fool Anyone!"*

**by
Wayne Allred**

**Illustrated by
David Mecham**

◆ A WILLOW TREE BOOK ◆

Published by:
Willow Tree Books
Box 516
Kamas, Utah
84036

ISBN 1-885027-04-4

Designed by David Mecham
Printed in the United States of America

This book is dedicated to
all those living out their country
fantasies from the comforts of
their very own condo.

Contents

Exercise Caution When Going Country

The Naselbys, a former "city family" turned country, were recently seen fleeing town with all of their belongings stacked on top of their Volvo station wagon. Just a few short months ago, they had come to the country with their heads filled with dreams of an idyllic cottage; a goat on the roof, chickens and ducks in the yard, and the smell of fresh air in their noses. Now here they were, running away, trailed by bleating goats, flies, the family dog (Lurch) and assorted skunks and vermin. Go figure.

Another acquaintance of mine, Max Larvington from California, suddenly felt a similar urge to "go country." He bought himself a pickup, Justin boots, Wrangler jeans and a cowboy hat. He scanned the radio dial until he managed to find a station in Nevada that, while it faded in and out, played good country tunes. He probably would have been dismissed as just another Kook from the land of fruits and nuts if he hadn't made the mistake of wearing his hat and boots while roller blading at the beach. Tragically, Max was arrested for lewdness after a life guard, who only had a rear view of the affair, believed he witnessed him opening his full-length, leather cowboy overcoat in front of some 4th grade neighbor girls. (He was really only reaching into his inside pocket to share his canister of chewing gum, but try telling that to the rest of the thugs in the jail.) Sadly, he failed to survive even one night in the slammer.

I tell you these stories not just to frighten you, but also to increase your awareness of the dangers of trying to play "country" without proper training and supervision. Countrying is serious business.

These Country Desires are Natural

Of course, scientists have known for some time now that most "normal" people are born with a powerful drive to return to their country roots. This is related to the human sleeping reflex and is nearly as compelling as the urge in 40-year-old males to dress like a geek and go hang gliding. Some people, like the Naselbys, while following this natural urge, have made attempts to live in the actual country. Others, like Max, have taken what they figured was a less risky approach and returned to the country without exactly "returning to the country", if you get my drift. Succumbing to this compulsive drive, some of them have done some pretty desperate things often with tragic results.

We can't fault folks for wanting to live the way that God intended. Their heart is definitely in the right place. But, many of them have so few country skills that they need the equivalent of 20 lifetimes of expert country help to have a snowball's chance in Phoenix of succeeding. Since I have spent a good deal of my spare time thinking about this country phenomenon, and since I can read at nearly a 5th-grade level, I have decided that I'm probably as qualified as anyone to declare myself an expert and write a book on the subject. I feel a very bold statement coming on:

A Very Bold Statement

Even <u>YOU</u> can be a country person! It's true. I believe that if you buy this book, assuming of course that you were born and raised in the country and had generations of ancestors who were real country people, or if you are a city person who has had a major physical renovation such as a brain transplant, nearly anyone can successfully go country. Here is where I probably separate myself from the real experts. I believe that even if you are a died-in-the-wool city person, even if you have never even been to the country, in fact, even if you doubt you could locate the actual country if it stuck to your boots and tracked all over your clean city carpets, with this book fully paid for and clutched tightly in your hand, I believe you can become country enough to fool a high percentage of city folks, and, failing that, to provide some good entertainment at parties for the rest of us. Also, I should note that this book, while not providing too many hard scientific facts or a great deal of practical data, will be chuck full of words of all kinds.

The Country Trend

Getting back to this "country" trend, taken as a whole, most country people would probably conclude that it's not such a bad thing. It has helped our self-esteem to have half the world copying our behavior, which we always knew was trend-setting. But there are some potential problems that we must address.

Take for example, growth. Even our little town is growing. And some of the growth is definitely a result of artificial, first-time country people, like the Naselbys, mentioned earlier, who moved here from the city to experience their own version of country living. Country people who are already here, have mixed feelings about these people moving in. On the one hand, they like the idea of their property values rising, and having someone to sell their diseased livestock to or play practical jokes on. But, on the other hand, some are concerned about having to be careful where and when they scratch and spit. Some ponder having to start buying hunting licenses and driving the speed limit for the first time. Others fear being forced to file for building permits or having to go clear back to the house just to use the bathroom.

So, it's natural that country people are so vitally interested in this trend and, also, because of a recent rash of failures, just a bit uneasy. Since I have declared myself the foremost expert in the field, I can speak with some authority when I say that having your horse step on your foot can really hurt and that allowing skunks to move under your house is a bad idea. Therefore, if you are a city person who is considering such a move, may I suggest that you hold your horses. You will find this book clear full of things that you will want to consider before you make a move that you might regret. Then your decision to live out your country fantasy, while staying put in the city, will be much easier.

The Wannabe Country Persons'
"Should I move to the Country?"
Test and Brain Scan

If the above discussion, (along with the knowledge that your country neighbors might be smoldering with resentment at you and your millions of buddies who are cluttering up their country landscape) has caused you to be a little insecure about your decision to move to the country, we have prepared this simple test to help you figure out if this is the thing that you should do. Mark each of the following questions either "Yes" or "No". If you are completely honest in your answers, you could end up with information that's every bit as useful a solar powered flashlight and as accurate as a presidential poll.

1. Is indoor plumbing something that you intend to use regularly?

2. Do you currently have a close personal relationship with anyone of another species; a horse, cow, dog, skunk, miscellaneous rodent, mosquito, or spider?

3. When dining in a fine restaurant, do you ever order Rocky Mountain Oysters?

4. Are you handy? Can you take appliances such as toasters, blenders, and tractor transmissions apart and the put them back together and have no major parts left over?

5. If one of your neighbors asked you to "throw a calf" could you do it all by yourself without help? How far?

6. Last summer, when some no-account city-bred imbecile severed your cable with his lawn edger, and you were without your TV for nearly 3 hours, did you become irritable, pacing wildly around while scratching your scabs until they bled?

7. Is good reception important to you?

8. If pressed, could you tell the difference between a cow and, say, an elk or a lung fish?

9. Is your idea of fashion tall, black, rubber boots, coveralls and a flannel shirt?

10. When driving in the country and you pass a feed lot or dairy, do you writhe in agony, screaming at the top of your lungs, and do your eyes water so much that because you can no longer see the road, perhaps causing you to bounce off from a telephone pole and land upside down in the ditch?

If you answered "yes" to more than 8 of these questions, while we aren't sure exactly what it means because some of them were designed for a "Yes" answer and some for "No", and we're still not sure which ones are which, we are certain that you should definitely take a very long and hard look before you consider moving to the country.

Another Approach to Deciding

Another popular method of evaluating an important decision like this is to use the "Ben Franklin" or "Gomer Pyle" approach. This is done by selecting a piece of paper from the floor of your pick up, and then carefully wiping the horse biscuit off of the paper onto your Wranglers. Then you write "Pro" at the top of the page on the left and "Con" at the top of the right. When this is done, you list the reasons in favor of moving to the country under the heading "Pro" and those against under "Con". Then, after carefully weighing the "pros" against the "cons", you ignore the hard facts and do what you want. For your convenience, we have done all of your thinking for you and prepared the following list:

Pro: Your career will receive a much needed shot in the arm because people will now understand that because you are a rural person, your word is as good as your bond, that you understand the meaning of hard work, that the reason you look so weird is because you are the eighth generation in your family who has married someone as closely related to you as your first cousin, and that you live in a house that has been in the family since your great aunt Maude had it built as an ad-on to her chicken coop in 1862.

Con: Because wages are substantially lower in rural areas than they are in the city, in order to make ends meet, you will need to take on a few part-time jobs, of which there are plenty, provided you enjoy butchering dead animals, shoveling out corrals and picking fruit.

Pro: Your kids won't wear pants that drag on the ground, shave the sides of their heads and dye the rest of their hair purple, spray-paint walls, get in gunfights with rival gangs, or use dirty needles.

Con: If your city kids do try wearing pants that drag on the ground, dying their hair purple, spray-painting walls, getting in gunfights with rival gangs, or using dirty needles, your friendly country neighbors will exhibit "tough love" by tenderly using them as drags to help smooth out the rodeo arena, or for target practice.

Pro: You will never have to jog or do aerobics again as long as you live, if you don't want to, and you can eat beef or pork, or any other dead animal that you choose, even if it is so full of fat that grease drips down your arms...and no one will even notice. And if they do, they won't care.

Con: You probably don't really want to.

Pro: You can drive any type of vehicle you want, no matter how old, ugly, or rusted out, and no one will notice because it will always be covered up by a thick layer of brown dust. You can also dress however you want, and say whatever is on your mind. It's expected.

Con: Even if you ever have a nice car, it

will look like it is 20 years old because it will rapidly become dented, the windshield will always be broken, and it will become covered by a thick layer of dirt within 30 seconds of the time you wash it. And your neighbors will generally always be feuding with you because, just like you, they usually say just what they think.

Pro: You may be able to revive your sagging musical career by changing from Rap, or Head-Banger music to Country-Western.

Con: You didn't have enough talent to make it in Pop music, and so the country crowd won't like you either.

Dang. I've run out of "Pros" and still have a few "Cons" left over. Consider these:

Living in the country means that you will have to entertain your own kids. I know you think you already do, but you don't. You have no idea how little time city people spend doing things with them. Think back to the last Christmas holiday when the kids were out of school. After sitting at home for 36 hours as an entire family, you wound up sending the kids to grandma's for the last 5 days, even though she wasn't home. Before you move out here, be sure you like each other.

You need to know that a wide variety of varmints also call the country home and they don't like to share, except for your food and bed. That means that you will be visited regularly by such critters as skunks, bats, porcupines, snakes, raccoons, rats, I.R.S. and insurance agents, flies, mice, mosquitoes, and very large spiders, and you will be expected to be neighborly. They feel that they have as much right to be here as you do.

You should know that sometimes the fresh air is "fresh" kind of like Rodney Dangerfield, especially if you live anywhere near a dairy or feed lot. Some guys say this is the smell of money. Maybe, but you might think it's more like the diaper pail from Hell. The only money I ever knew that smelled like that was stuff my buddy Bryce fished out of the bottom of the outhouse down at the fair grounds.

Expect your driving routine to change too. Instead of running here and there in your clean, little car for 5 or 10 minutes, you will need to begin to plan to be on the road for half of your life. And your nouveau baby poo brown car, which was once candy apple red underneath the dust, now only gets washed when you drive under sprinkler end-guns.

Another irritation for you novice country persons, is the amount of time that must be factored into your lives for visiting. When you go to the store to pick up some milk, Earl will want to tell you about his arthritis. When you go to the post office to drop off the bills, Alice will chat about her kids. When you go down to the filling station to get gas, Gus will bend your ear for a while about politics, and so it goes. Gone will be the days of making a priority list of things to do and then just doing them. Out here, getting one meaningful thing done all day long is doing pretty good.

Finally, you will need to fix your own stuff when it breaks. Although there is a mechanic in town, and although he charges half what a city mechanic does, he is very thorough (meaning slow) and it can take some time to get your car fixed. Plan on up to a decade under normal circumstances, assuming that you are like most city people and don't have good visiting skills yet and so you don't bother the mechanic. Otherwise, buy a new car.

And, if something else breaks down like say, your air conditioner or your water pump (yes, city people, you will have your own well and pressure pump, holding tank, septic tank and miles and miles of plastic pipe), you will just have to fix these yourself, just in case you ever need water.

So, you who are thinking about moving to the country, here is some food for thought. Consider your decision carefully. Don't make us spend the next three years trying to figure out what made you want to leave, like we are having to do with the Naselbys.

Once the Decision has Been Made

If after careful consideration, you have decided to be a "city" country person and forgo your move out here, choosing to live out your country fantasy in your condo, for the most part, we have said all that we need to say. You can go now. If, on the other hand, you have concluded that yes, in spite of the fact that you will be much happier if you stay where you are, in spite of the fact that your kids will be much happier staying where they are, and in spite of the fact that we country people will certainly be much happier if you stay where you are, you still want to be an actual country-located country person. If you are saying to yourself, "I know that this makes absolutely no sense whatsoever. I know that I will make everyone including myself, miserable, and despite the fact that I am doomed to failure and will probably be eaten by a wild animal, I want to be a country person." If this is what you are saying to yourself, you can count on us country folk to "Cowboy Up" and do our best in a true country hospitality sort-of-way to support your decision and help you experience first-hand our country sense of humor. Read on.

Buying Your "Spread"

Every true country person needs a spread. (country for "farm" or "ranch") So, if you truly want to become a country person, acquiring a spread should be one of your highest priorities. 100,000 acres or so is best. You will need lots of ground to "ride those little doggies", or for the buffalo to roam and the cantaloupe to play.

Now, of course, we realize that there are many of our readers who may not be able to afford 100,000 acres, especially if they happen to be operating on a sanitation engineer's budget in a place like Orange County California. So, if you can't afford 100,000 acres, with some planning, you can still be a bonafide country person with only 100 or so. You will just have to do without quite so many wide open spaces, and a few less doggies, buffalo, and antelope.

I realize that for many of you who, through no fault of your own, are "capital disadvantaged" (or C.D.), even 100 acres may be a cost-prohibitive hardship. Fortunately for you, there are other options that can make a person feel just as "country" for considerably less money. For example, in many suburban areas, there are cute little 1 acre "ranchettes," which actually bear some resemblance to an artificial imitation of pretend country living, only without so much of the dirt and inconvenience. People who have a whole lot more money than you do can sometimes afford to buy one of these. And while even if you could afford this option, you still probably wouldn't have many buffalo roaming or antelope playing, zoning laws will, however, sometimes allow you a rabbit, sheep, dog, or tank of tropical fish. And if you really go country and keep some good clutter around the yard, you may be able to coax a skunk or some other forms of wildlife to hang around some.

Finally, I know that while most of you would like a big spread like those mentioned above, it just may not be in the cards. No matter what, the best you can do is a rented condominium. Don't be discouraged. Poverty and poor judgment should never thwart you in your quest to become a real country person. Many well-known country people nowadays live in condominiums. If I had the time,

I could probably name a few, but trust me. There are many truly country-like things that you can do in a condominium...and no one will be the wiser.

How to be Country in a Condo:

If you find yourself in this position, like many people do, and you are forced to live out your country dreams in a condominium, you will need to follow these simple instructions extra close to have a good experience:

First, for the rest of your life, you must never be caught without your boots and hat. If you can manage to wear these two essential country items everywhere you go; at work, to the symphony, in the swimming pool, people will perceive you as either a country person who, due to events beyond his or her control, is trapped in this uncomfortable, restrictive, urban environment...or they will just figure you're some kind of a dork.

Second, speak with a drawl and continually cuss...and spit. This may take some practice, and even some strategy, at least the spitting part if you work in a high-rise office building, because some bosses and managers frown at cussing and almost all hate spitting. But if you are really country, you're tough enough to deal with this. Ignore them. They're just jealous.

Third, you must have some animals. If your condo project has prohibitions against horses, get yourself a dog, hamster, or chicken. This feeling of having livestock around is essential to maintaining that country bearing and attitude. And even if all you can manage are some really small animals like roaches, laboratory rats, or, heaven forbid, a cat, they will need some kind of scratch box. This is good. It has an added side benefit. You can pretend that this litter box is your "range." I have seen some trapped, urban country people even go so far as to dress up their scratch boxes with little plastic farm animals, cowboys and Indians or matchbox cars. (Real country folk naturally use matchbox pickups.)

Fourth: Eat red meat and enjoy it. If any of your city friends give you a hard time when you're out and about eating at restaurants and they're all eating tofu and you try to order spotted owl in beef gravy, just cuss and spit. They will get the message.

Fifth: Carry a 3 inch, round canister with you everywhere you go either in your Wranglers or your shirt pocket. (In point of fact, it doesn't really mater what 's in the can. It can be carrot sticks, twinkies, or even horse biscuits for all I care, but it is vitally important that you always keep a wad of whatever it is under your bottom lip.) This is necessary to impress all of the city girls and boys. *A word is in order here about chewing tobacco or "snuff" as it is sometimes called. If you should choose to chew actual tobacco instead of trendy alternatives such as sugar-free gummy bears or trail mix, you need to be aware that tobacco is real adult-type stuff. If you have never tried it before, it's not the kind of thing that you can sneak up on or ease in to. So, if this is your first time chewing and spitting, do it right by following these instructions: Grab as much as you think you can hold in your mouth. Then stuff it in there using both hands if necessary, and start chewing real fast. After about 10 seconds, take a deep breath and swallow the entire mouthful quick, in one big gulp. If you're not used to chewing, this will give you a genuine appreciation for it quicker than anything that I know of. Some veteran chewers season their chew with tartar sauce or salsa to help it go down. And many lady chewers like to add calcium supplements or iodized salt to reduce the risk of osteoporosis and goiter in later years.)

So there you have it. Don't let anyone tell you that you can't be a real country person just because you can't afford a large spread. It is still possible to be a country person, even in a condo. Just follow these common sense guidelines and you will be held in high esteem by yourself and other judgement disadvantaged (J.D.) neighbors. And just maybe you'll fool some honest to goodness city people too.

"Yep, stainless steel!"

Meeting Your Neighbors

We all know how important a first impression can be. I believe it was the famous adventurist and big game hunter, Ralph Nader, who said, "You never get a second chance to trim your nose hairs with a weed eater." While this doesn't have much to do with your country neighbors, we believe that it is still sound advice. We also think that you should spend a lot of time worrying about the impression that you leave with your new country neighbors. And there are many reasons why this is important. When you live in the country, you need friends for all kinds of reasons; to borrow things from, to pull your pickup out of the ditch, to put out the fire in your house, and to help you catch animals that get out.

-23-

Here are some tips that you should follow when meeting your country neighbors, if you want to leave a lasting impression:

1. Everyone loves a sincere compliment. Go on and on about what a fine spread they have. (If it's a condominium, make a special fuss about the litter box as previously noted.)

2. Pay special attention to your neighbor's animals. Even if you're not sure exactly what kinds of animals they are, even if some of them have big sharp things sticking out from the sides of their heads, walk right over next to them and get acquainted. This show of confidence will impress your neighbor. He will naturally assume that you are completely comfortable with animals. In the event that this is a big lie and in fact you are terrified of and totally unfamiliar with animals, in order to not embarrass yourself, we have prepared a few catch phrases for you to use to disguise your ignorance. Use as many of these as you can in the course of the conversation:

Catch phrase #1 "Whooee! What a nice bunch of geldings you've got pardner! You know, I'm looking for a sire for some of my barrows and gilt's. What do you charge?" *One important note: If you're not exactly sure if his animals are male or female, you don't need to let on that you have no clue whatever. Just be patient and your opportunity will come to find out for certain. The best way to subtly determine sex in an animal is to loudly and repeatedly use the word "Bobbitt" in the animal's presence. Then carefully watch the expression on it's face. If the animal starts to squirm and even covers his ears, you can be fairly certain the animal is a male.

Catch phrase #2 "I've got a couple of head of doggies over at my spread that are getting mighty dirty. If you shake yourself loose for a few minutes, could you drop by and sit on them while I hose them down?"

Catch Phrase #3 (Since all country people, even women, will think you're an idiot if you're not familiar with farm equipment, use these catch phrases to fool them about your lack of experience): "Is that a D-47 over there? I was just out the other day on my F-16 discing under a circle of garbanzo beans that caught a bad case of the nematode." I've always favored DeLaurean tractors over Chrysler or Isuzu, what is your favorite?"

By using these catch phrases, you should be guaranteed a memorable first impression when meeting your new neighbors.

Tips on Horse Shoeing for Beginners

Since owning horses or other animals is an important part of your transition from city to country person, but also can be complicated if it's your first time, we have started for your benefit, a group called The Society of Advice about Pets, (S.A.P.) to help teach all of you new converts important facets of critical animal maintenance. Our motto is "an ounce of prevention is worth at least the price of surgery for replacement of a lacerated kidney."

One of the biggest challenges for someone with little experience in horses can be shoeing his horse for the very first time. It's true, new horse owners, during the winter time, in order to avoid equestrian frost bite in the hooves or having your horse catch his death in cold, your horse will need good, warm shoes. (At least, until springtime comes again when you can let the little rascal run barefoot again if you want.) Here, then, first time horse owners, is what represents many years of experience in applying horse shoes, which I figure is worth it's weight in dandruff.

First, once you have determined the type of horseshoes for your horse (see below), you must get your horse into the proper position to apply the shoes. You have probably noticed by now that horses are very large animals, some weighing nearly as much as Roseanne Barr, and the kind that you really don't want stepping on your foot. One of the biggest problems with inexperienced horse owners is that they try to apply shoes while the horse is in an awkward position, often standing up if you can imagine, with the horses leg bent up in an unnatural position. By doing this, they subject themselves to the risk of dangerous horse-stepping-on-toe-type accidents plus they annoy the horse. We recommend applying shoes to your horse while the animal is lying flat on his back with all four feet in the air where you can see what you are doing.

There are two tried and proven methods for getting your horse onto his back in this manner: First, and the easiest way that I have found, is to try the old trick of engaging your horse in stimulating conversation while one of your friends sneaks around behind your horse and kneels down on the ground. Then, when he least expects it, give your mount a hard shove with both hands on the chest and he will fall right over your crouching friend onto his back.

My editor is poking me with his ruler right here insisting that this might be a good time for the old "law suit-deflecting disclaimer" So here it goes: **WE ARE NEVER RESPONSIBLE!**

Also, this appears to be a good time to mention an important safety tip: Do not leave your friend crouched behind the horse's tail for extended periods of time. Bad things often come out of that end of your horse.

In the event that the above method doesn't work, another proven way to get your horse onto it's back, especially if you are an in-experienced cowperson, is to use some kind of "horse relaxer". You can do this by going to your dentist and borrowing some of his nitrous oxide or "laughing gas". Most dentists are happy to let you use their tanks as long as you tell them that you're planning to use the gas for horses only and if you reassure them that you would never even consider using them when your friends come over to play cards this weekend or to perform maxiofacial surgery without proper training. After he gives you the tank, you put a bag of oats around your horse's mouth, poke the hose in there and before you know it, he will be feeling no pain. Be sure and watch his eyes closely, and of course, you want to be sure and get out of the way as he goes down.

With your horse lying on his back, you will need to work quickly to apply the shoes since nitrous oxide has interesting side affects on some animals (My neighbor's horse woke up believing he was a wolverine.), and because, if you used the "pushing him over your crouching friend" method, he might be peeved at you. Oh, and be sure that he doesn't drive or go in swimming for at least an hour afterward.

Moving quickly, the easiest way we've found to apply horseshoes is to use super glue. The draw back, though, is that if you let your horse up too fast, they glue won't be dried, the shoes may fall off, and you will end up starting over again. If this happens, I can guarantee you that this time your friend will have a tougher time sneaking around behind your horse. (If gluing doesn't work and you end up nailing the shoes into place out of desperation, whatever you do, don't let the animal rights people find out about it.)

Concerning the type or "style" of horseshoes, there have been a couple of exciting new developments in horse shoeing recently. The Birkenstock company now has an alternative to traditional horse shoes. They have a slip-on that is so easy to use that it can be applied with the horse in an upright position. It's so new, that I haven't had time to try it out, but I've heard that all you do is slide the little leather strap over the front of the hoof. I've also heard that it only works with California Horses.

There you have a few useful suggestions for shoeing your horse. If we had more space, we could also explain about equestrian dental maintenance and removing an appendix, but we'll save those for another day. Happy shoeing!

Many Lessons Can Be Learned From Owning Animals

One tried and proven way that many parents use to help their offspring grow up straight and tall, which we country parents all instinctively try at some point, is to get the kids an animal. Like all faithful parents the world over, my wife and I have periodically followed this strategy. Now, after four kids and many years of being in the pet business, I believe that we are in a position to begin to evaluate the true effectiveness of this particular parenting strategy and its influence on our kids. The following is a brief run down of the lessons that we have learned from owning "pets".

The first lesson that we planned for our children to learn was "R" for "Responsibility". This was to happen by having them take care of a horse. We knew they would grow from the daily responsibility of having to feed and water the animal, and then chase it out of the alfalfa patch and off the highway. This responsibility, combined with the knowledge that without such diligent attention, this wonderful friend of theirs would go hungry and thirsty and eventually die, we knew would be highly motivational to them. How critical that a child learns to be totally committed and one-hundred percent faithful in performing a task! What a shame that my children will never learn this valuable lesson!

Mom and dad are, however, learning much about diligence and responsibility. After all, somebody has to cowboy up and feed and water these miserable varmints. The kids have way too many other responsibility-teaching activities like little league ball games, 4-H, soccer practice, homework, spells of amnesia, homecoming week, birthday parties, and fatigue to worry about animals. Mom and I are grateful though, because we have become much more responsible than we used to be. When those animals need to be fed, we feed them. When they need water, we water them. When they haven't been ridden for so long that they're ready for the rodeo, we ride them. We are much better parents for the experience.

Next, we were confident that by owning animals, our children would develop an understanding of the value of "M" for "Money".

We remembered how OUR parents insisted that WE manage our livestock and treat it as a business, making them produce economically. In order to learn this lesson, we let our kids take pigs to the fair. We fully expected that our own children would learn such useful concepts as the value of money, the thrill of earning their own way, and the satisfaction of knowing that their annoying pig is finally in someone's freezer.

After a few years of FFA and 4-H pig projects, at least the wife and I have a clear understanding of the cost of owning animals. We know what it's like to have gut-wrenching depression-like hard times, feeding our own children rocks cooked in water, holding up 7-11 stores, and intimidating 2nd graders for their lunch money, so that we could keep pouring pricey, top-quality feed into the all important pigs so they would make weight.

Finally, one of the lessons that we wanted our children to learn was "C" for "Compassion". We had hoped that by caring for a puppy, these higher paternal and maternal instincts would be cultivated and their love and appreciation for all of God's creatures would begin to swell up inside them until their little hearts would nearly burst. That's SORT of how it turned out. They did manage to get better control of their mouths after we washed them out with soap and water a few times for sounding like little sailors since they had to spend time with those ##!*%#!!!@$! pig-headed animals who do such irritating things that one wonders how anything can be so stupid and live. On the bright side, although my wife takes issue with this, I swear that sometimes, if I listen ever-so-carefully with my heart, and not my ears, I can detect an occasional faint flicker of love and compassion in the children's voices as they scream and argue with each other over whose turn it is to feed and water the animals. So the experience hasn't been a complete loss.

Summarizing these terrific lessons can best be done by putting the first letters of all of these words together: "R" for "Responsibility", "M" for "Money", and "C" for "Compassion. If we do this, we will discover that they spell "RMC", which as near as I can tell doesn't spell anything, and which is about what we figure our kids have learned. It could, however, stand for "Run to the Marine Corps", which is a terrific place for a kid to learn many of life's lessons about Responsibility, Money, and Compassion...Well, maybe not money or compassion, but at least, they would learn something, which is much more than what they are doing with all of these critters. If I sound a little cynical, it's because one day when the kids had been particularly irresponsible to the point that we were sincerely concerned that the Humane society would be by any day now, we had a discussion about getting rid of them (the animals, not the kids). As we discussed each pet by name, the children tearfully saw the wisdom in trying something else, and agreed to let them all go. But when it came right down to it, it was the Wife and I who just didn't have the heart...except for the pigs.

"If after these detailed instructions, you're still confused, hopefully the following carefully documented descriptions of real country living will help you decide if you are really cut out to be a country person."

Guidelines Must Be Followed When Dropping Off Pets

Times have really changed. We truly live in a kinder, gentler society now than when I was a boy. Thanks in part to gentle reminders and the threat of litigation hanging over our heads from animal rights advocates, most of us are even starting to be kinder to our animals. We're not supposed to eat them any more, or at least, if we do, we're not supposed to enjoy it. And we're not supposed to use their excess body parts for things like shoes and fur coats or bow and arrow targets. Political propriety now demands that we shouldn't be raising animals for any of the purposes for which they have been traditionally raised. Instead, we should be using all of that feed grain for things like booze for human consumption. Then let all of our animals run wild and free eating our Uanamus bushes.

A big part of this "kindness to animals" trend is the movement away from old fashioned methods of pet control. I'll bet you can't remember the last time someone admitted that they took a bunch of kittens or puppies up to the canal in a gunny sack. Me neither. Living away from town like I do, I see evidence everywhere of this trend of people being more kind to their animals. By the thousands, they are now choosing to take the humane way out and drop their unwanted animals off out in the country for me to take care of, instead of taking them to the target range or canal. Dozens of new stray cats show up in my barn every day and a virtual plethora of stray dog varieties and packs run through our property each night on their way to eat one of the neighbor's sheep or calves, wild and free, as God intended.

Yes, it looks as if our farm yard is a popular place for modern humanitarians to humanely dispose of their unwanted pets. Most of the time we don't mind being the repository for the whole world's unwanted animals. But I must confess, that at rare times such as when a starving, rabid pit bull chases my wife up a tree, or when the whole family comes down with ring worm from one of these unvaccinated stray cats, I get a little peeved. For this reason, I feel it my duty to inform the public, that if they feel that they must drop off their unwanted animals near my spread, that they follow these few common sense rules:

First, be sure that the animals are well fed. The other day, I went outside and a pack of extraordinarily bony-looking dog-like creatures had just taken my 8-year-old son down and were finishing off his snow boots and parka, and appeared to be getting ready for the main course. I was able to coax them from our yard with some dog-biscuit-shaped rocks and then encourage them to proceed to our neighbor's place (who incidentally has commented many times on how much he enjoys taking care of hundreds of unwanted pets). I know, the humane thing to do here would be to have fed them some T-Bone steaks from our freezer before sending them on their way, but I was having a bad day. And since you can never be sure that when YOUR hungry former ex-pet shows up around my place that I won't be in a surly mood, please feed your animals before dropping them off in the country.

Second, be sure that they are friendly. There is absolutely nothing worse than a strange pet with an attitude. An example of this might help to illustrate my point. Not long ago, I was outside weeding my garden, when a gang of abandoned dogs were taking turns spray-painting my fence posts in true dog fashion with doggie gang slogans and then admiring each other's work. When I walked up, stick in hand, to keep them from further vandalizing my place, they all turned on me like I was the one who stole their girl friends. They bared their collective fangs, growled, and circled around me like they were about to attack. Fortunately for me, Earl was plowing his carrot field next door and as he was coming close to my place, his 1959 John Deer did a couple of consecutive loud back-fires, which startled the gang so much that they scattered, probably convinced that their rivals, the Snoop Doggie Bloods were making a drive-by shooting. I was probably lucky to get out of there alive. Just imagine what would have happened if I had happened upon a doggie gang initiation or drug deal. I would be sleeping with the fishes.

And finally, be sure that your abandoned pets are properly neutered. I know that this is a subject that most of us don't want to talk about, but these changing, difficult times call for extreme measures. Before you drop off your pet, you absolutely must exhibit "Tough love" and have them "modified". If you're not willing to do that, at least take some time and explain to the little animals the risks of their promiscuous behavior. Otherwise, each spring we wind up with dozens and dozens of little baby critters running around getting eaten by the starving bigger critters. And we haven't even begun to discuss the effects that these animal public displays (P.D.A.'s) of affection have on my young children and the excruciatingly difficult questions that I am then forced to answer before I'm ready. Some of these canine's do such disgusting things in public that would make Dr. Ruth blush. And when I think of the terrible health risks that these critters are ignorantly exposing themselves to, I cringe. Most definitely, a frank discussion about safe sex is needed before you drop your pet off out here in the country..

So, there you have it. Although I get the warm fuzzies thinking about this trend of kindness to animals, I must confess that I am only a recovering carnivore and I ate bacon the other morning for breakfast and enjoyed it. There. I feel better after coming out of the closet. But as you can see, I still have a ways to go getting used to treating animals better than humans, but I sincerely want to do my part and continue to be the receptacle of all of the worlds unwanted pets. Please, though, do YOUR part too and follow these few common sense rules when dropping off your animals.

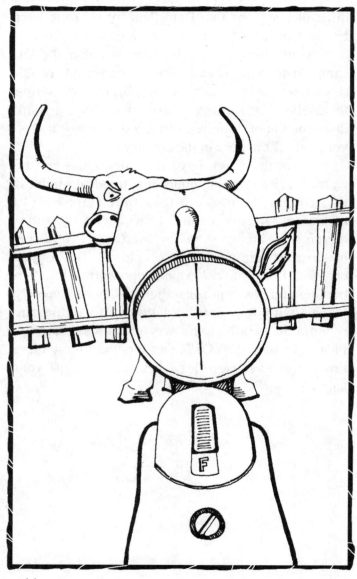

Lets Start Using Idioms and Save the Planet

Now days people don't talk to each other as much as they used to. Most of us spend more time talking to our computers than we do to other people. The art of good communication seems to be dying out. Part of the problem is time. We don't seem to have enough to waste on being sociable, visiting, or explaining what we really mean. We rarely even have the time to explain important things, like what caused the cat to explode or how come the kids were all painted blue when we came home this afternoon, let alone common, boring stuff.

Fortunately, some of the older generation are still alive. They can remember when people could really communicate. If they were to look up from their TV game shows and try to talk to us, although it would be hard for some of us to understand at first, they would probably use a type of speech now largely forgotten, that we used to call the "Idiom." (From the Greek word "idiot", used by the ancients to curse their animals, and which means "to lie")

The question in my mind is, why don't **YOU** use idioms when you talk to **YOUR** children? Why do we modern people just grunt or yell? Do we want our kids to grow up with a mutated view of life? I don't think so. I think the problem is that we have actually forgotten how to use idioms. We no longer remember how to uses phrases like; "A belch in time feels fine" or; "A penny saved is a miracle."

The good news is that it's not too late to change. And if you are a parent, you will want to change quickly. In my mind, it's no coincidence that the decline in use of good language parallels the drop in young peoples' respect for their elders. I'm convinced that if we are going to bring back that respect, we must return to the tried and proven methods of communication that produced the generation that developed space exploration, genetic research, Richard Nixon, Gilligan's Island, and pet rocks. In fact, if we are to have a chance at heading off the imminent destruction of life on this planet, we must begin today to use the forms of speech that so engendered respect in young men and women for their elders. Of course, I'm speaking about threats of corporal punishment and the monotonous drudgery of honest work, but I also think it would help if we could add some color to our usual alphabet soup acronyms and boring computer-eze by using a few idioms.

Let me explain why I believe reviving the use of colorful language will cause respect to grow and save the planet. When you were young and couldn't understand what your grandmother was saying, you automatically figured that she was so much smarter than you that she understood and you didn't. How would you feel right now if the younger generation had no idea what **YOU** were talking about? Wouldn't that be wonderful? They would probably figure you were some kind of computer technician, rap singer or nuclear scientist. With that in mind, I have prepared some new "modern" idioms just for you. By randomly sprinkling these about in your speech, you can get great respect from your kids, your spouse, and anyone else for that matter. Some of these idioms are so deep that virtually nobody will get them and so naturally, everyone will conclude that you are one smart cookie. And of course you are.

The next time you notice your children's respect for you start to decline, try slipping one of these into your conversation:

"The most beautiful flower in the world will kill you if you snort the petals up your nose."

"Trucks with chains on shouldn't be allowed to park on people's feet."

"A hairy cat burns bright."

"Having to spend a week being audited by the IRS makes one appreciate the sensation of being dragged through a swamp while chained to the bumper of a truck all the while being attacked by Africanized bees."

"A turkey that knows how to bark has a decent chance of surviving Thanksgiving."

"The long trip to the ocean begins with a small flush down the toilet."

"When the rats move in, the roaches move over."

""It's hard to dodge the seagull poop when

your eyes are glued to the pavement."

"Politicians are like roaches. It's not that they eat so much, they just contaminate everything they touch."

"Whenever you see your hound lift his leg over the nitro glycerin, dive for cover."

"If you insist on hanging around with urinals, expect to get soaked."

You can shave your hamster if you want, but don't expect him to look any better."

"If you don't want your clothes to smell like a septic tank, don't play cards in an unventilated room with cigar-smoking people who have gas."

"Politicians are to virtue what a squid is to a helicopter."

"If you drive through a red light fast enough, you can make it seem like it's a different color."

"It's easier to get eggs onto a paint job than to get them off."

"You normally don't notice that your

neighbor's feet stink when you have your own boots off."

"Putting your head in a microwave oven most likely won't clear up your complexion...and it may even make your teeth fall out."

"Don't shoot the bull in its tender parts with your pellet gun unless you're certain that the fence is really strong."

"You can brush your teeth with a horse biscuit if you want, but it won't improve your social life."

"A truck load of dead worms will put off a whale of a stink."

"Whenever you pass a cop, be sure to check your seat belt."

"If I never finish building the addition onto the kitchen, it can never catch on fire during the night and spread to the butane tanks near the fire place which would engulf the bedroom portions of the house in flames and we won't all die."

There now, don't you feel nostalgic? Can you imagine how much better the world would be if we all talked like this? Go ahead. Try these idioms. You'll become the wonder of your friends and children, and you might even save the world as we know it.

DESIGNER
PET PIG
COLLARS

by CALVIN
SWEIN

*"For Those People
Who Treasure Their
Porkers"*

*Also See
Our Fine Line of
Bacon Bracelets*

Pig Economics

I could easily argue that Pigs were economically the most important animal in the development of this country. (I could also argue that my pet duck is a computer programmer, or that middle school teachers are going to stop wearing pocket protectors. But then that would put me in a category with some people you know who will argue about anything. And since there is already enough conflict in the world, let's stick with today's subject of the value of pigs.)

You may not be aware that pigs were among the first animals imported to the Americas, arriving with Columbus on his second voyage. Pigs multiplied so rapidly that they became very common. They were everywhere in colonial

America. Their pictures were even on the first coin minted in North America, Bermuda's silver piece.

Pigs are resourceful. Until most recent times they have usually not even been penned up, but have been left to fend for themselves in orchards and woods. In spite of this irresponsible lack of adult supervision, these so called latchkey porkers have done nicely. When the first settlers to America wanted some pork, they could usually get it by heading into the forest with their gun on their shoulder and shooting one of the many pigs that were there.

Moreover, nothing on the pig was wasted by our ancestors. They needed lard for a multitude of uses such as candles, soap, and pranks like greasing up the doorknob to the old outhouse. They used the hide for shoes, belts, harnesses and footballs, and the ears for silk purses. And, of course, they ate everything edible on the pig including some pretty disgusting stuff that we shouldn't mention in a family newspaper.

As you can probably tell, I have great respect for pigs. Not only are they economically important, but as an added bonus, they are great teachers of young people. Why, just the other day, I was with my sisters at a family reunion. We were waiting for the gates to a water park to open so that all of the young cousins could rush inside and see who could be the first one to crack open his head and get stitches. Since we had 15 minutes or so to kill before the place opened, I was making small talk with my youngest sister about her work.

It turns out that a young man from the town where we live, who we will call Kimball, had recently begun work at the "city" business of my sister. She went on and on raving about what a good worker this guy was and how mature he was for just an 18 year old. She then questioned me about growing up on the farm and what it is that makes country boys so wonderful.

"It's the pigs," I replied.

"What?" asked my sister.

"IT'S THE PIGS!" I shouted louder over the noise.

At that moment, our conversation was drowned out by the hysterical shrieks of a female police officer who happened to walk by us and who was screaming in my direction something to the effect that if I'm ever lying on the highway bleeding, she hopes that there are some pigs around to rescue me. I quickly concluded that she must have been a city police officer who probably missed some of the conversation. It's also possible that my sister, who never did hear my explanation of the effect of pigs on young people, is still standing there to this very day with a confused look on her face.

Anyway, pigs do build character. It's true.

A perfect illustration of this is the case of my 14 year old daughter, Erin. This year she took a pig to the fair to show. Every time Erin ran into someone at the fair who would ask her what she was showing, she would say a horse, goat, fish, or hamster. She swore that she would never be associated with a humiliating, disgusting pig. Then she got her check for the sale of her animal. Now the discussion has changed to what is the best business structure (partnership, proprietorship, or corporation) to use when she sets up her commercial hog operation.

Yes, thanks to the pigs, my adolescent daughter has learned a vital adult lesson. Now, deep down inside, she knows that she will willingly do disgusting and desperate things for money.

And this is just one example out of many. If this column wasn't so short, I could give you hundreds of other examples of how pigs and their friends, cows, and chickens, can help change your child from an ear piercing, heavy-metal listening, beer-swilling, drug taking, drive by shooting, adult-hating, hormone encrusted lunatic to a responsible, intelligent, mature, pig-raising, milk-drinking, smiling, and good-looking young person, but I think that you probably get the point.

And now aren't you glad that you have this new appreciation for the economic as well as the character-building nature of pigs? And, aren't you glad that if you should ever happen across me when I have been in an accident on the road, that you will immediately stop and help?

Amazing Facts About Your Pet That May Give You Indigestion

1. If you were dead, your cat would probably have no qualms about eating you.

2. Children who grow up without the benefit of being around dogs tend to have better table manners than apes in the wild.

3. Dog observers insist that there are over 460 things that your pet dog will do only once. These include: Falling asleep on the freeway, peeing on an electric fence, getting a drink out of the toilet when it's being un-plugged with "Plumber's Helper", and chasing a dangling high-voltage wire.

4. Given the choice, a normal pig will choose to eat

ice cream covered with dog food and maggots over brussel sprouts.

5. Chickens seen at the bottom of the cistern will often require CPR to be kept alive.

6. One woman, Maude Cloister, once collected the loose dog-hair from her couch, clothes, and vacuum cleaner. After only 4 years she had enough to provide all of the batting in a camp quilt.

7. Rabbit droppings taste nothing like the raisins they often look like.

8. Normal cats don't swim underwater.

9. Ervin "Spud" Ogilvie of Othello, Washington had a fetish about furry hamsters. He shaved his pet, Ralph, every day for 5 years until it froze to death.

10. If you took all of the mice and grasshoppers that a common garden snake eats in a year and put them end to end, you would have a string of disgusting, digested organic material long enough to spell occipital across four lanes of freeway.

11. People have long debated which farm animal is most intelligent. People who work with any of them know that if all of their collective brains were

rabies virus germs, there wouldn't be enough to infect Lincoln, Nebraska.

12. Sally Bergwald of Kalamazoo, Michigan once fed her pet gerbil a diet of straight vinegar, baking soda, and Sugar Free Dr. Pepper. After 2 months, its behavior became very eccentric even for a gerbil.

13. If you drop a cow from an airplane at 10,000 feet and it lands on its feet, even if its udders are full of milk, it won't bounce very high.

14. Experts tell us that you could fit more than 11,000,000 earthworms inside a Volvo Station Wagon, many more if they are dehydrated.

15. Alvin Grizwold of Bend Ore. set a Euness World Record for a 200 pound man when he rode his pygmy goat, Bea, 875 feet before it collapsed from fatigue.

16. Scientists tell us that wild turkeys cannot fly as fast as the slowest BB from your 12 gauge shotgun.

17. Contrary to public opinion, it really is possible to pull a flying frog behind a beer truck, provided you can find a way to get its tongue to stick.

18. Studies show that if you sleep in the same

sleeping bag with a skunk or porcupine for an extended period of time, your ability to get a date with a human of the opposite sex diminishes exponentially.

19. Even after you have pulled all of a Wolverine's teeth, you still have to use caution to avoid getting bitten...but if you do, it won't hurt as bad.

20. There are few practical, economically viable commercial uses for frogs.

21. If you use a vacuum cleaner to milk your cows, you can expect them to be harder to catch the next time.

22. Mel Perdley of Peoria, Illinois proved that it took his pet blow snake, Betsy, 18 minutes to down a small chicken. He could, however, cut the time in half by giving the snake regular electric shock.

23. A blue whale eats enough plankton in only one day to completely clog the toilet of an average Winnebago.

24. If termites could eat rocks, people would be more nervous about climbing cliffs.

25. In recent years, rats have been able to develop an immunity to almost anything. However,

scientists have been unable to raise rats capable of surviving being run over by earth-moving equipment.

26. If all of the insects who have ever lived were to die suddenly, most people would be uncomfortable walking barefoot.

27. Earl Spindley of Rupert, Idaho found that he could get his pet guppies to turn upside down by feeding them common dish washing detergent.

28. If you consistently feed fish to your rabbits, after just a few days their pens will begin to smell very bad.

Vermi-Sept™

An Alternative to Septic Tank Pumping

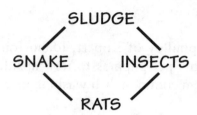

Just place the bag of Vermi-Sept Critters in
your commode, flush and stand back.
In only 2 to 3 months there will be no sludge,
insects or rats. . . just one very large snake.
Warning: The Surgeon General has
determined that neglect of the snake can prove
hazardous to guest commode users.

Vermi-Sept™

For Septic Tank Owners Who Are Truly Environmental

When your tank is full of fecal
and your field is smelling rank,
flush Vermi-Sept down the hatch
and let nature clean your tank.

Farmers Could Solve All of the World's Problems

In spite of the way we sometimes look, we farmers are a highly intelligent bunch. We are the world's premier problem solvers. Possibly the most amazing skill the industry has acquired is the uncanny ability to avoid physical work. If it is possible to have a job done with machinery, we'll figure out how. I have seen farmers who could rig equipment up to make a 10 minute job last an entire week, and that without hardly even working up a mental sweat.

I witnessed an astounding example of this special skill when I went over to the neighbors to help their daughter and her husband move the "heavy stuff" into their new home. While this other flunky and I were grunting and straining, trying to slide the freezer to the front of the truck, one of the real farmers in the group had already gone to get the heavy equipment: the front end loader. After he arrived, all we had to do was slide the stuff into the huge barrel and then be ready on the other end to scoot it into place. We hardly had to lift a finger, except to shovel out the fragments of the stereo system, China hutch and freezer we dropped. But that was nothing compared to the project we would have had moving it all by hand.

That's why I have a hard time understanding why this farming industry, which has been so amazingly efficient that farmers have literally invented and mechanized themselves out of jobs, doesn't apply it's skill to other, non-farming, aspects of life. It seems to me that if we could just broaden the agricultural industry's horizons, they would have a legitimate shot at solving all of the world's problems.

For example, how about having farmers devise a weight-loss program that would actually work? No one in this billion dollar industry has figured out a system that keeps weight off for more than a few weeks, except, of course for boring stuff like exercise and good nutrition which nobody in their right mind will ever try.

I suppose that one reason why farmers haven't taken this on as a project is because the idea of weight-loss is pretty foreign to people who spend their lives trying to fatten things up so we can eat them. But here, let me show you what I think would be a typical farm approach which I could envision: Let animal power do the work. Lose weight nature's way, organically, using intestinal parasites. What could be more natural? People in many foreign countries live their entire lives with a stomach full of them and they don't seem to mind at all...except it lowers their energy level and their life expectancy, and gives them all of the symptoms of chemotherapy...but we could work on these side effects.

Imagine a clinic where you walked in and the vet offered you a choice of 4 or 5 different capsules, each containing a different bug or worm. Then you could live your normal life, eating everything in sight because you would have a terrific appetite, all the while dropping 10 pounds a day. As soon as you achieve your desired weight, go back to the vet and get a shot of ATGARD to kill it.

Hey, I know this sounds disgusting, but compare it to binging and purging. Or compare it to an entire lifetime of torturous aerobic exercise and eating the Epicurean equivalent of wool socks for every meal. We could at least give people the choice. After all, this is America, land of the brave.

Another problem that I hereby challenge the agricultural industry to solve is the gang problem. I'm a pretty marginal farmer, so you know that the solutions that I come up with aren't prime stuff, but

I have a feeling that agriculture would propose
"heavy equipment" solutions like this: Begin at 4
in the morning during planting. Get all of the
members of the gang together, pry the spray paint
cans out of their fingers and take them out to the
field.   Then just put them on a piece of heavy
equipment...like a tractor. Let them drive it for 20
hours a day like young, rural homeboys do during
planting, until a couple of 120 acre fields are
planted. Next, give them a new piece of heavy
equipment like a hoe, and send them out for 12
hours a day hoeing weeds in sugar beet fields.
When that season is over, put them out on a digger
or a picker during harvest for 16 hours a day or
until the work is done.

Now, if, after all of this, they still have
energy and the desire to go do a few drive-by
shootings, give them a 22 and point them in the
direction of some jack rabbits or the neighbor's
cats. (I'm kidding! I'm kidding! I love cats!)

Now, I know that some of the powers that
be would be hard to sell on this and for some
legitimate reasons. For example, sometimes the
gang members would miss school because they
would be needed at work. We could never justify
having them use work as an excuse to miss school.
No, if they're going to miss school, it should only
be under the direst of circumstances like getting
busted for having automatic weapons in their
lockers or to make an appearance in juvenile court.

Another problem is that former juvenile delinquents would no longer be able to get money from the federal programs which up to now have been their economic life-line, because they would be making too much money driving tractor. They would no longer qualify. And of course they would probably just blow their money on drugs.

OK, so, maybe agriculture can't solve the gang problem, but maybe we could turn our farm technicians loose on the budget deficit, trade imbalance, teen pregnancy, world hunger, or my obsession with chocolate.

All the Action at Odd Hours of the Day Delivering Country Papers

Most people get so caught up in their own little world that they miss a great deal of the excitement and beauty of life that goes on around them, especially in the middle of the night. This is not the case with we rural paper delivery people and mail persons, however. We see and take time to enjoy things every day that would make a sailor blush. Because so many people never have the time to see the world as we do, we want to share the beauty, the excitement, even the cost of the damage to our cars with you, our readers. That's why I've been asked to take my recorder along and dictate things as they happen while on my route delivering papers.

So, here we are getting ready to go on

another exciting paper-delivering trip. First, of course, I have to check the oil in the car and make sure that all of my newspapers are in order. Now we're on our way. I'm backing out of the driveway onto the busy road.... same to you buster....where I live. Make a note to be sure and look both ways in the future so people don't have to swerve to get out of our way. It makes them angry and they might cancel their subscription.

Now, we're driving down the road, heading for our delivery site. It's a misty, drizzly day, about 38 degrees, really quite pleasant for delivering papers.

Here's my first house, the Fenortners. He has a baseball card shop in town, a son who is incorrigible, a daughter who isn't very cute and this big dog here that they call "Duke". Delivery people have to be careful here because Duke is an unusually sneaky dog who often times never barks or makes a sound until he has his teeth dug into you. And then he just sits there and growls the way he's doing right now until you can figure a way to release him from your arm. The best way that I've found is to take the cigarette lighter in your free hand like this and hold it just below his rear end like so...(By the way, Don't tell the A.S.P.C.A. people about this dog-releasing method or you may have to get a new newspaper person.) When it gets uncomfortable enough for him, he'll loosen his grip and "Voila!" you can get your arm out and drive away like we're doing now. One problem with starting at Fenortners is that you have to toss newspapers with your inside hand.

This next house just down the road a piece belongs to Stan and Mildred Weed. You can see as I pull up next to their mailbox that I have to be really careful because of these deep, deep wheel-ruts. And then, of course, there's that big ditch over there. If it's raining like it is today, if you don't keep your speed up, you can get stuck pretty good. The reason why we almost got stuck is because I'm not used to having to use so much of my brain to talk into this recorder, so I'm not concentrating quite as much on my driving.

By the way, I don't think they mind so much fishing their newspaper out of the mud where we dropped it. They have known me for a long time and they know I would never put it in there on purpose. Besides, I can blame their neighbor boy, Jeremy Stokes who lives a ways up the road and who spends a lot of time bothering the Weeds because they're kind of old and fun to play tricks on. He has to stay out of the house even if the weather's bad because his dad travels a lot and is gone for long stretches of time and... you see that pickup over there behind those trees? That's Don Millican's. He's generally over keeping an eye on Mrs. Stokes while Mr. Stokes is away. He's the one who doesn't like Jeremy around so much.

To be continued...

Excavation Unearths Important Information on Term Limits

Voters of late have stirred up a hornets nest by demanding term limits for our elected officials. The idea of term limits is very controversial. Recently the Congressional Resource Allocation Panel (C.R.A.P.) conducted a poll of Congresspersons and it found that more than 108% of the congresspersons polled were opposed to any kind of limit being placed on their terms in office. Other polls taken of average people show widely varying support.

The numbers often depend upon how the questionnaire is worded. For example, one poll which asked the question, "Do you favor getting rid of your honest, hard-working incumbent congressman and losing his influence, so that they close all of the military bases, electric plants, and businesses in your state, so that life as we know it ends and you have to go back to living in filth and ignorance and die of AIDS?", Only 94% said "yes." But when the question was phrased; "Would you like to have the choice to vote for someone besides that sleazeball who is getting rich from your taxes, provided other states were forced to have non-career politicians too, so you were not at a disadvantage?" As high as 99% answered yes.

This is truly a baffling issue that could be very divisive to our country. I can see all of the elected politicians lining up on one side and all of their constituents lining up on the other. And it could be a whale of a fight.

Wanting to do our patriotic duty and help find answers to this tough issue, and since we had recently obtained a federal grant to do research on pioneer diets and reading materials, we felt that we could combine our research on all three topics at once and still have the government pay for the whole thing. So we wasted no time.

While excavating the ruins of a bunch of old former pioneer outhouses, looking for reading material and evidence of what the pioneers ate, we discovered a well preserved, but slightly soiled and badly ripped article from the <u>Muskogee Democrat</u> dated Feb., 1824. Imagine our shock and surprise when we found that they were debating this very issue of term limits way back over 170 years ago.

We have decided to publish this article in it's entirety, (at least the entire part that we were able to salvage). It was in the form of a debate between one Senator Earl Muffinslinger, head of the local political machine, and a small-town reporter, Jed Kroppel. We hope that by observing how this issue was considered years ago, we can shed some light on this difficult and confusing topic and help you decide whether or not YOU support term limits.

The complete, un-abridged text follows:

Mr. Kroppel: "Senator, All due respect for your position, but I feel that if you just had to be a normal, non-Senatorial, voting person for a while and choose between holding your nose and voting for a candidate who's values are diametrically opposed to your own, and who is a corrupt, self-aggrandizing career politician, because he had been in Washington for so long that he knows every freeby, influence peddler, power broker and brothel, but who could, because of those connections, give you special favors and protect your special interests against the overriding concerns of the entire country,.....or choose a new, innocent, fresh face, who, if you elect him, the powerful allies of your former representative would use their influence to destroy the economy of your state, that you would either become nauseous on election day or else quit voting out of sheer disgust."

Sen. Muffinslinger: "The constitution already

provides for a way for you to remove unwanted politicians: The voting booth."

Mr. Kroppel: "But, your honor, elections as they are now are not a fair contest. A challenger has no chance against an incumbent who has received years of free publicity during his term in office, who has name recognition, who uses his office to pay-off those who support him by passing legislation favorable to them, and who has the ability to raise many times as much money as an unknown challenger and who often uses his staff, to make sure that he gets reelected."

Sen. Muffinslinger: "If ignorant, shortsighted, unethical journalists like yourself want to elect some reprobate child-molester, who will steal their wallets, and who will cost everyone within the voting district their jobs, they can do that right now without imposing term limits,...through the voting booth."

Mr. Kroppel: "Many people feel that public service should be just that, "public service." They feel that the type of person who runs for election for a brief period of time, because of a sense of public duty, is fundamentally different from a person who is in it for the money and a long-term career. Many feel that we would get better service from people who were not career politicians."

Sen. Muffinslinger: "I can't believe how little ethics you press have. You're all crooks and muckrakers. In fact, you, yourself, are probably a convicted felon. I'm sure that if I knew enough about your personal life, I could ruin it like you're trying to ruin mine because of some personal vendetta....

The scrap of newspaper that we found was so badly soiled from here on that we couldn't read any further. But, hopefully, the part that we were able to decipher will help to shed some light and give insights into this difficult and perplexing question of term limits.

The Experience of Buying a Horse

Abe Browning was in a tight spot. Old Bessie, his faithful mount, who had served him for years and even carried him across an entire continent, had finally given out. The creature had reached the point where one thing after another was beginning to go wrong. First, her feet had become so sore that she refused to walk. After expensive foot repairs, including new horseshoes that cost $8.00 with mounting and balancing, she had only been back on the road for a couple of days when ominous rumbling noises began emanating from her stomach. The horse began to balk. It was in too much discomfort to even walk, let alone pull a plow. And then there were those sounds coming from the rear end that Abe knew would eventually mean even more trouble. Reluctantly, he took her to the vet again, who, after an examination, gave him the bad news that the cost of fixing his worn out old nag would be more than she would be worth afterward.

This meant that he was faced with a difficult decision; whether to stuff her full of sawdust and then try and pass her off to some greenhorn as being less than 5 years old, or to light her on fire, push her off a cliff and try to collect the insurance. Before resorting to such desperate measures, though, he wanted to see what he could get in trade.

Abe liked shopping for horses about as much as he enjoyed being dragged naked through a cactus field or having his face worked over by a sado-masochistic wrestler with a power sander. He would rather face a firing squad. But he knew there was no alternative. Having no better idea about how to begin, he gamely rode into town, sneaked into the first livery stable he came to, and started looking at the used ponies that were tied up there for sale, all of the time hoping against hope that a salesmen wouldn't spot him and come running out. He wasn't ready to have his arm twisted until he had a chance to look over the stock.

Luck wasn't with him. A salesman, wearing a lively synthetic fringe-leather plaid jacket and loud pants, bounced out of the back room and walked right over. The man asked if he could use any help, and before Abe had a chance to answer

"No", he found himself being led to a group of horses that he could tell from clear across the lot would be way out of his price range. Even though he only shops for horses every few years, Abe recognized the sales tactic of showing the fancy mounts first, in order to make the cheap stuff seem crummy by comparison. This first horse was a late-model mustang with low mileage and one owner. It had a sleek, real leather saddle with power stirrups and way more pep than Abe needed just for chasing around the farm. Abe shook his head, "No".

Next, the salesman, brought out this good looking Palomino. But good LOOKING was all it was. No matter how they tried, they couldn't get the stubborn thing to move.

The next horse was a large, healthy Appaloosa. It's eyes made Abe nervous. They were a gray-white color and the horse didn't move it's head when things in front of it moved. The salesman said that most guys who worked around machinery preferred a horse who couldn't see because they didn't spook so easy. But Abe wanted to look some more.

As Abe tried to leave, the salesman said he had one more horse that he had to see. Even though Abe knew this was just part of the routine, and that the salesmen like this weren't really human and therefore never felt rejection, his sense of good manners overrode his desire to flee. Besides, he couldn't tell the salesman that he was in no hurry to buy, because his trade-in was now lying in the street with her feet in the air drawing flies.

Aside from the sway back and limp, and the fact that the animal's teeth were worn down, this last horse really didn't seem too bad. Besides, buying a lemon horse, when compared against having to face another salesman was no contest. Abe took the bait.

"How much would it cost me?" He asked. While this seemed like a simple enough question to Abe, apparently the notion that a prospective buyer might want this particular bit of information had never crossed the salesman's mind. "Make me an offer and then I'll go inside and try to sell the manager on it", The salesman said. Taking the man at his word, Abe made him what he thought was a fair offer. "Just relax here on this bale of straw. I'll be right back." said the salesman.

"Right back" obviously meant "right after the next solar eclipse causes worms to grow teeth." because it was hours before he returned. Worse than that, he came back with a funny look on his face. Wouldn't you know that Abe had chosen the only horse on the lot that the boss really didn't want to sell. He had planned on keeping it for his kids. But after the salesman held his breath for half an hour, he finally agreed to let it go. He did, however, want considerably more than Abe had offered.

And so, not wanting to offend the man's

sensibilities, Abe made another "best offer" and then waited patiently for the salesman to return..., then another..., and another. Hour dragged after agonizing hour as the salesman bounced between Abe and his boss. Finally, long after closing time, when everyone else in town was asleep and all of his manly pride had been brutally squashed to powder, Abe was at the point where he would have agreed to trade his entire family for a lame skunk. He knew that he would agree to sign his own death certificate if they would just let him go home.

And then, quicker than you can ride across the Gobi Desert on a skateboard or knit a set of curtains for a 30-story office building, his credit was approved. And as the sun began to peek over the western hills, another contented new horse owner proudly rode a shaky new mount back to the farm to show the misses.

Newspaper Delivery Action: The Next Day

The following adventure is continued from last night when our hero and narrator grappled with dogs, traffic, the elements, and his own limitations as he doggedly performed this vital service to mankind....

Because of all of the problems, we were able to deliver papers to only 3 homes last night. Sometimes this job is like that. So if we're going to finish this paper route before next week's edition comes out, we've got to make better time than we have been making. Today, we're going to put our little car into newspaper delivering warp speed and really hustle. Because we're having to hurry so fast, I'm going to do something that I learned from the post office, which we delivery people only do in an extreme emergency: We're going to sort of skip some of the houses. Don't worry. It will just be the ones that don't pick up their paper every day. This is OK for newspaper and mail persons to do occasionally since some customers don't even notice. And, since we're doing this narration, this move will leave us more time to show you the real interesting people on the route.

By the way, those flashing lights behind us belong to Steve Green, the local county mountie. He and I are pretty good friends. He just pulls me over like this sometimes to give me a hard time because our city-league softball team is better than his, because I married his high school sweetheart, and because I drive down the wrong side of the road, run stop signs and violate most traffic laws while delivering my papers when I think he's not watching. So he goes to great lengths to surprise me. He sure did this time.

"Hi Steve, how ya doing? I know my license plates have expired. I know I was driving down the wrong side of the road. I know I ran that stop sign. And I know that guy back there ran off from the road, but that accident wasn't my fault. Besides, you know about the newspaper deliverer's creed, Neither rain nor snow nor traffic laws will keep the paper person from his appointed rounds. Heh heh."

I've always wondered if it wouldn't really be faster if I did my route on foot. An added benefit of doing it this way is that if I deliver newspapers for a couple of hours each day, I will get myself into superb cardiovascular shape. Besides, the old car was on its last legs. Steve thinks he got a real bargain with it, but it will cost more to fix all of the problems than the darned thing will be worth afterward, especially if you add the cost of the impound, ticket and towing to the tab.

Yes, doing the route on foot gives a person the opportunity to really stop and smell the flowers, to truly enjoy life as I mentioned at the beginning of the article. That's why I think I'll be doing it on foot for a while now.

The house that I was hurrying to before the interruption was this one here. It belongs to the Schmurtzs. Sometimes you can hear them arguing way down the street. There's even another benefit of being here on foot. I can sneak in to their porch quietly without them knowing I was here so I won't be the one that gets accused of turning them in to the State Family Services people. Actually, it was Mrs. Bernheisel up the street who did it, but no one is supposed to know because Mr. Schmurtz would probably come after her with his gun after he finished shooting the social worker.

That's a 30-06 he's packing and I have to whisper while I'm hiding in these bushes because if he finds me, he would naturally assume that I had just witnessed him throwing his 3 year old son through that window and swirling his daughter's head in the toilet and in that case he could very well use the gun on me, which would be a real tragedy because then they would have to get a new newspaper delivery person and this route wouldn't be done for weeks.

It's looking like I could be here for the duration of the night waiting for an opportunity to sneak out of here and finish my route, so I'm going to turn off the tape. We can always finish tomorrow night.

To be continued...again...

Taking Girls Horseback Riding While Understanding Women

Throughout my entire life there has been only one brief window of time, around age 17, when I was really certain that I completely understood women. Even then there was still one thing that I didn't understand, I could never figure out why girls never seemed to enjoy outdoor adventure as much as we guys did. Every time we would ever do an outdoor activity, they would whine the whole time.

"Whining won't help," I said to my date, Rhonda. "If you're ever going to learn how to ride horses, you have to start by learning how to put on a saddle. Here, slow down and let me explain again. The mistake that you made was getting on the horse without first cinching up those straps there." I could tell that she was at a point where she really needed a hug of affection. And I was just the guy to give her one too, if I could just catch up to her.

"Whoa now!," I said. "Pretend that you are doing your aerobic incline sit ups. Use a burst of strength to sit up and grab hold of those reigns flapping in front of you. If you can manage to give them a tug before you pass out again, maybe you can slow the horse down enough for me to catch up and pull your foot out of the stirrup."

I wasn't sure if she could hear me because her ears, nose, and mouth were completely full of dirt from being dragged around the corral. But then I saw her groping in the correct direction for the reigns and finally grabbing onto one. "Good job!" I exclaimed, "Now pull hard." She did, and finally old Bessie slowed down to a trot, a walk, and then finally a complete stop.

It wasn't long after that that the two of us were on our way. We were double-dating on a horse back ride with my buddy, Reed, and his date, Mary Ann.

"There you go whining again, Rhonda" I hollered. "Just lighten up. Somebody has to ride Small Change and you have the shortest legs." I couldn't understand why she was complaining when, after all, she was in the wide opened spaces with some handsome guys. Summoning all of my patience, I explained: "A Shetland really is best for you because you're new at this and you don't have so far to fall. Besides, you can stand up whenever you lose your balance without the horse getting away."

The trail wound through the scrub oak-covered low foothills and at first it was easy going. But then, after an hour or so, it began to get exciting. "Rhonda!", I hollered, and I had to yell loud because by now she was a long ways back there, "What ever you do, don't look down when you get to this trail dug way." The trail crossed a huge rock slide for about three quarters of a mile. There was a 1000 foot vertical drop that I liked to spit off from just to watch it sail out of sight. I don't know about you, but to a 17 year old boy, having a girl leap 20 yards from sitting on a half-a-horse and then cling to him like an octopus to a rock was about as romantic as it gets. This was true even if the girl was wearing dirt for make up, had all of her back teeth chipped from bouncing so much, and had been sweating profusely for 3 hours. Me and Reed took great pride in our organizational skills. We had every detail, right down to this scary part of trail, planned to perfection.

A while later, we reached the previously determined destination and went right to work prying the girls off from our necks so we could have a romantic noon meal around the camp fire.

"Looks like some things are missing. Let's go over the checklist one more time." I instructed

Reed: "Pork and beans."

"Check."

"Peanut butter."

"Check."

"Pop corn."

"Check."

"Milk Duds."

"Check."

"Ketchup."

"Check."

"Pop...Reed, you forgot to pick up the pop! Oh well. Never mind. We can drink out of the crick like God intended. You girls get the grub out of the packs while we men gather fire wood."

While we were getting ready to build a fire, the girls began complaining again. As I looked at Rhonda, she seemed to be crying, although it was hard to get a good look at her through the black cloud of mosquitoes swarming around her head. I guessed that she was a little saddle sore from the way she dragged her legs along the ground behind her using just her arms. She was being a good sport though, as long as no one reminded her that we had to ride all the way back the same way we came.

"Quit worrying about those mosquitoes," I said again. "We'll get a fire going and you can put your head in the smoke to get some relief." I have to confess she looked a little comical with splotches of blood dribbling down her dirt-caked face where she had squished mosquitoes.

While I was rustling through the pack, looking for the non-existent repellent, Reed was yelling at me to help him find the matches. After an hour or so of trying to start a fire with everything from two rocks to two sticks, the girls were finally so tired that they said they didn't care so much about dinner. So we guys got the peanut butter out and ate it with our fingers.

Since we had to get the girls home before dark, we knew it was time to break camp and get on our way again. But before we did, it would have seemed sacrilegious if we didn't take just a moment to savor the great outdoor atmosphere.

"It just doesn't get any better than this!" Reed exclaimed. And you know...I think he was right. That's why I just can't figure out why even now, as adults, when we go on these camping trips, the girls are still always complaining.

Rural Newspaper Route: The Third Day

If you remember from our previous two days, we have only been able to finish delivering newspapers to a total of five houses in three days because of a set of bizarre and rare circumstances, delays and problems. Hey, didn't I tell you that delivering papers was full of action and adventure? In any case, because we are so far behind, we still have two thirds of our route to finish in only one day, so we've got to hustle like never before. I am forced to take drastic measures and borrow my grandma's car in order to finish this route.

I'm getting in the car and backing out into...same to you jerk!...the road again. I would like to make a note that today the sun is shining brightly, but the wind is blowing gusts between 10 and 85 MPH according to the weatherman. You readers should know that adverse weather conditions like these can make delivering newspapers much more challenging, even more challenging than say, removing your own spleen with only a fork and a pan of boiling water. That's why only America's finest are chosen to carry the cellulose and the canvass. Getting this many papers delivered today will demand some creativity developed from my long years of experience.

Our first house today is the Jacksons. They don't have a newspaper box, so we just toss their paper up onto the porch like this...this...this...this... Don't worry, I always bring some extra papers along when it's windy. I am also trained in emergency aerodynamics. I can fold newspapers into large paper airplanes and then sail them literally into these stiff gusts of wind and make them land on the porch...OK, maybe not exactly ON the porch, but within the same zip code. There are, however, some days when the wind is blowing the paint off from cars, that no matter what you do, you just have to get out of the car and walk up to a few porches and lay the newspaper down where it belongs. Then the problem often arises, how to get the paper to stay on the porch. That's where we experienced newspaper people have an advantage over laymen. We know how to hold the paper down with one hand while we dig a hand full of mud out of the flower garden with the other hand like this and then put it on top of the newspaper to hold it in place. This looks like about a 7 handful day. Then we walk quickly back to the car and never look back. That can be bad luck.

One problem with having to get out of the car at every house and put a pile of mud on top of the papers is that it takes a long time. So on days like this when you're in a terrible hurry, it's important that you have some other alternative ways in mind to get your newspapers delivered. I am about to show you how a veteran newspaper technician makes "Mister Wind" his ally instead of his enemy. An ingenious way of doing this which I have used on rare emergency occasions like today, is to find a spot up-wind from an entire row of houses. I then pull my car up onto the curb, stand on top of it, and let fly one paper for each house, like so. The wind will carry them closer than you could ever throw them. The only problem with this strategy is that some of your customers will have a hard time finding all of the pages to their paper. They forget to look in the paper-catching bushes of their neighbors, down wind. And of course a good paper boy will help solve this problem by throwing a couple of extra newspapers up into the air to provide "spare newspaper parts" for the ones that are lost. You have probably figured out the added side benefit of using a whole bunch of newspapers as extra parts like this; namely that you can get through A whole route in just a few minutes.

Thanks to ingenuity and using our heads, we're almost finished with the route today and in record time. In fact, it took us less time than many of our customers will take gathering up the parts of their paper. We do need to make one final stop though. All newspaper people and mail persons know that the route is never complete without a stop at the local greasy spoon to hang out for a while and sort of unwind. I usually like to stop in at Earl's, depending upon whose cars are out in front. Those are the cars of a number of my customers.

Well it looks like I don't really have time to stop today because I just remembered that I promised my wife that I would trim my nose hairs and pet the duck. Those people in there look angry! See you again soon!

"Well, you can kiss that ball *goodbye. . .*"

Country Summary

.∂. Here, then, are a few suggestions which we feel can help you in your quest to go country. You now have some tough decisions. The information in this book should have given you some definite words to read. (Or at least some more pages for you to put in the old outhouse to take some pressure off from the Sears catalogue). What you do with this information could leave a lasting impression on many sick and diseased animals, your future pets, and possibly even some friendly country people.

You know now that countrying can be tough business and is definitely not for the faint of heart, uninitiated, and anal retentive. Hopefully, this book has impressed upon your mind some of the risks of going country. After all, who wants to wind up a miserable failure, or even dead in a California jail cell? Probably not you. As you consider these important decisions, remember the words of Abraham Lincoln or some other famous guy, who once said, as he rode through the countryside sounding the alarm, "Ask not what your country can do for you, ask: Do I really want to trade city utilities for an outhouse?"

Order these additional books
by Wayne Allred

  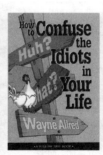 

Willow Tree Book Order Form

Book Title	Quantity	x	Cost / Book	=	Total
			$6.95 US		
			$6.95 US		
			$6.95 US		
			$6.95 US		
			$6.95 US		
			$6.95 US		
			$6.95 US		
			$6.95 US		

Do not send Cash. Mail check or money order to:

Willow Tree Books   P.O. Box 516 Kamas, Utah   84036
Telephone 435-783-6679
Allow 3 weeks for delivery.

Quantity discounts available. Call us for more information.
9 a.m. - 5 p.m. MST

Sub Total =	
Shipping =	$2.00
Tax 8.5% =	
Total Amount Enclosed =	

Shipping Address

Name:

Street:

City: State:

Zip Code:

Telephone: